Against All Odds

Building My Empire Brick by Brick

Nikki Relford

Just a girl from Maida with a dream that refused to become a statistic!

Against All Odds:
Building My Empire Brick by Brick

Nikki Relford

www.NikkiRelford.com

ISBN: 979-8-9857151-6-3
First Edition: January 2023

This book is dedicated to every person with a dream. It is my prayer that you find the strength to push toward your dreams no matter what you may face along the way!

<u>Contents</u>

__Acknowledgments__

Rewriting a book is harder than I thought yet more rewarding than I could have ever imagined. None of this would have been possible without my book coach, Shana Booker. She was exactly whom I needed to assist with my project. I'm thankful for her editorial help, keen insight, and ongoing support in bringing my book to life. From conception to fruition, we made it happen!

To Mr. Nick, owner of Spartan, who took a chance on a stranger back in 2011. I am forever grateful that I was able to open my official first business location inside your Spartan Auto Sales. You motivated me to push forward and seeing your success made me believe that I could accomplish my goals also. Thank you for introducing me to things I never imagined like starting a dealership. I realized that I didn't need to have all the answers. As long as I was coachable and knew how to utilize my resources properly, I could do anything, so I thank you.

Writing a book about the ups and downs of my life was a surreal process. It required vulnerability as well as courage. My desire was to focus on the obstacles that I've had to conquer to get to where I am in this present moment. One of the biggest misconceptions is that success comes easy but that is farthest from the truth. In the pursuit of success, there is guaranteed to be pain and hurdles along the journey.

I must say thank you so much to my daughter, Alyssa Carry for riding shotgun on this crazy roller coaster we call "life". I became a mother at the age of sixteen, but I never allowed that to stop me from providing you with the future I wanted you to have. It was because of you that I worked hard, never gave up, and fought through the most difficult times in my life. I never wanted you to experience the things I had so I vowed to create a life for you and your brothers that I could only dream up. With that being said, I hope that you are proud because against all odds...we made it.

To Aunt Lisa, thank you for always being the person I could turn to during those dark and desperate years. She sustained me in ways that I never knew I needed.

To my brothers and sisters, thank you for never being short on encouraging words and always believing in me.

To my husband and children, thank you for allowing me countless moments to be selfish with my time. It has allowed me the ability to perfect my creativity on a level I can't even put into words. I realize that affording myself time to be selfish is a great sacrifice for you and it does not go unnoticed. I thank you immensely. Through it all, just know I really do have a plan amid the chaos.

Last, thank you Mom for always providing and showing us what hard work consists of. You are the epitome of what a real boss is. Through your actions, I learned that I could reach any goal I set for myself through hard work and dedication.

To my readers, this is the beginning for some and a pitstop for others. Whichever path you may be on, just know that I am rooting for you! Trust yourself and take it one step at a time.

Please check out my handles below for the latest news, booking speaking engagements and products:

Email:Admin@NikkiRelford.com
Web: www.nikkirelford.com
Facebook:
www.facebook.com/nikkiunderconstructionrelford
Instagram: www.instagram.com/author_nikkirelford

INTRODUCTION

Selfless Love...the greatest form of affection that one can display: agape selfless love specifically. It amazes me how in the twentieth century we have all the tools and tricks to understand life and how to power through with our higher self, but only utilize a fraction of it. Have you looked at social media lately? Everyone under the sun has given themselves permission to carry self-claim titles such as "doctor", "philosopher", and "mentor" to name a few. Why do you ask? My analytical take on things is that healed people heal people. I'm extremely optimistic and prefer to look at the glass half full rather than half empty. There is something deeper that people can cling to when the person counseling them has been through a similar storm as the person seeking guidance. In the youthful days of our parents and ancestors, making it to see the next day was pure joy and a mission accomplished. While that sentiment continues to hold truth and value, the newer generation requires a bit more "coddling". If I could paint a picture for you, I would say we, collectively, represent the Amazon package that has the big red stamp labeled. "FRAGILE. PLEASE HANDLE WITH CARE". The misconception of this analogy, unfortunately, many people weren't taught not to equate gentle with soft. Teaching individuals that being in tune with their feelings and self-worth is a negative connotation will reap massive destruction as it has already been shown to be true thus far in the world. Children as young as ten and eleven are committing suicide for various reasons, but mainly due to a lack of love and understanding. I don't proclaim to have all the answers, but I do know from personal experience that a lack of the most innocent, freeing, and plentiful emotion you can show someone will wreak havoc on a person's physique and how they view others in the world if it is lackluster.

As I've mentioned, I have endured my fair share of trauma when it relates to choices made during my adolescent years. I did not grow up in a home that overflowed with warm and fuzzy vibes. However, it doesn't mean my parents loved me any less than the next person. My cards were simply dealt differently so we were more like "The Evans" and less like "The Huxtables." It was to be implied that my parents loved me based on the unspoken expectations that any parent should adhere to when accepting the role of guardianship. At the tender age of fifteen, am I supposed to praise my parents for feeding me each day? Keeping a roof over my head? Putting clothing on my back? I mean, let's face it...saying "thank you" is a great gesture since we teach our children at a young age the importance of verbalizing the phrase, but realistically no one expects an underdevelopment mind to grasp the magnitude of how noteworthy it is to tackle such obstacles daily without soliciting help from others. Parents don't always notice when they are falling short in a child's eye; especially when they are focused on making ends meet. So yes, you may have gone through some days where you wanted to hear "I love you" a few more times than you got. Charge it to their heads and not their hearts. This is where grace is extended. The vast majority of the world typically repeat what they witness in their childhood, especially if the person deems it normal. It is a must that we do our part in breaking these generational curses. Doing nothing is contributing to creating more hurt people that will hurt people. It's scary to think that however love was packaged in your childhood is the same type of love you will probably seek in your adulthood. Recognizing that love can be painful, finding your happy place can seem like a battle. According to an article written by Darius Cikanavicius, "…you [could] fall madly in love with the perfect partner to discover later, and only too late, that they are an illusion. You may find yourself tolerating behavior, pain, and unhealthy displays of love and affection that you notice other people don't." How does that make you feel? Does it sound the alarm and make you think about choices that you've made in the past or currently making? It surely helps me to somewhat understand why I made certain choices in my life.

Close your eyes and imagine lying on a beach with a drink in your hand while the sun gives you just the right amount of rays and the wind tickles your scalp ever so gently. Now imagine the aroma from a Japanese Kobe steak dancing in your face when the waiter removes the silver dome covering your food only to reveal trash dripping in delicious butter. I don't know about you, but I've never been a fan of eating out of the dumpster. It doesn't matter how you dress it up in your mind, trash is still trash. This was the analogy of my life for quite some time. I've hit the peaks of mountains and ran low as valleys. My life was a rollercoaster, and I was forced to participate in it.

Let's be clear, this is not a book meant to be bashful nor am I setting up a platform to critique the shortcomings of anyone. I am merely stating how rising above my adversity propelled me into living out my ancestor's wildest dreams.

Hello readers! My name is Nikki Relford and I am a woman with a purpose and a plan. I chose to stand up and fight back against everything that was meant to destroy me. I'm a country girl at heart, born and raised in Beaumont, Texas. I am one of multiple children which contributes to my nurturing side. I have a passion for children and a take-charge attitude. From the tender age of sixteen, I've been in a position of management. Being able to excel in high-pressure positions catapulted me into entrepreneurship. I learned that I could get the job done by any means necessary and I'm damn good at it! I currently have a few different successful businesses under my belt including the ownership of a daycare and a girls group home. In addition to my businesses, I have an amazing husband whom I adore and seven children (four biological) that I couldn't see my life without. When the days seem dark, they are truly my refuge.

Now I would be remiss if I only shared the glory but didn't shed light on the story. It is my hope that this book will help people going through turmoil in their life and/or searching for some type of motivation that they could gravitate toward to help them cross the finish line. Truly grasping the understanding that a changed mindset will break chains beyond your measure is extremely gratifying. As the old saying goes, to get something you're never had, you must do something you've never done so let's get into it!

No one said life would be easy, but if you move to your own beat...it's worth living. Waking up is the hard part. Now that you've survived another day, what do you plan to do with it?

xoxo
Nikki Relford

Chapter

Love Jones

The Sweetest Thing I've Ever

Known.

He was like "the perfect verse over a tight beat" or whatever Dre said to Sidney in the movie *Brown Sugar*. Everything that I never thought I would have in my life, he showed up as. He was a comforter. He was a provider and a confidant. Most importantly, he was a friend. I needed him more than he realized, but not for what the typical teen was in search of. I needed to be rescued from this harsh reality called life. It was like the brother hijacked my mind and morphed into everything my young mind desired.

When my boyfriend met me, I was in a fragile state of mind. I was trying to find my balance as a seventeen-year-old mother to an innocent and beautiful baby girl. While her smile brightened my days, it didn't change the fact that I felt alone, lost, and confused. I felt like I was a failure because raising a child while being a child was not in my plans, nor my parents for that matter. I understood why they were upset about my actions. Hell, I was trying to keep my own composure while juggling a slew of emotions including frustration, hurt, and depression. Despite everything, I was hopeful that the emotions would subside, and my parents would come around. I held out hope for the day that my parents would offer up a much-needed hug, kiss, or any words of encouragement. I needed to know that everything was going to be okay. The gut-wrenching part is that day never came to pass. What I did receive was negative opinions from others cast upon my life. I hid my feelings extremely well and no one thought the wiser. Instead, a fighter was born. I refused to become a statistic nor was I going to allow my daughter to become one. I vowed right then and there I was going to beat the odds and rise from the ashes like the phoenix. I aspired to prove everyone around me wrong and I set out on a mission to do just that.

I started working a full-time job to provide for myself and my daughter. Soon after, I picked up a second job to assure myself that I had enough funds for everything we needed and some of what we wanted without help from anyone. Instilling that mindset into my new way of thinking is what drove me to always have my own back. The caveat to this newfound strength was the hindrance to progression it would later cause in other aspects of my life.

Aside from my beauty, my strength is what captured the eyes of my boyfriend. He knew he had a real one on his side. We dated for the remainder of my high school year which was great. He was loving, caring, and protective. He accepted my daughter and cared for her like she was his own. We were a family and for the first time in a long time, I felt at peace. After graduation, we decided to make it official and get married. We were young children in love trying to find our way in this world like everyone else. Life was going smoothly, and we were high on love. It couldn't get any better than that or so I thought. A couple of years after we tied the knot, we purchased our first home. We looked good on paper. We had the American dream…love, marriage, family, and the white house with a picket fence. I was in hog heaven as the old folks love to say. Our bodies and minds were in tune with one another. Often times, we could sit in a space together for hours without saying a word, but the room never felt cold and empty. It also felt warm and loving.

As our life continued to elevate, I was propositioned with a new job opportunity which was amazing, but the training location was not ideal. I would be required to train out of town. After some careful consideration between myself and my husband, the offer was accepted. Even though out-of-town training would be short-lived, we didn't want to lose the closeness that we have spent so much time creating. To help bridge the gap in distance, we made sure to check in with each other often while I was away. Upon my return, I was blown away by how immaculate the house looked. Everything was clean and put up in its proper place. The aroma of a home-cooked meal swept me off my feet. Internally, I was thanking God for blessing me with my husband. The royal treatment didn't stop there. He continued that pattern for quite some time. My husband made sure to accommodate me in every way possible when it came to helping around the home and being in tune with my feelings. After training, I started working at the new company and it was going smoothly. I couldn't complain. I was in a good place emotionally and financially. Life was great or so I thought.

God has a sense of humor that is challenging to appreciate when we're in the middle of a storm. We don't understand the full picture until we look back on it. Some of the people God sends our way are for entertainment only. We must stop taking the tags off returnable items. The great thing about God is that He will step in before we go too deep into the water. Have you ever been running late for work and you're trying everything you can to get there quicker except nothing is working? You've tried going around granny that's moving at a speed of 60 miles per hour in the fast lane when she knows that the right lane is her friend. You've tried speeding through a few yellow lights only to get caught up by a train or some sort of construction. You honestly can't figure out how you overslept because you laid down at a decent hour and set four alarms. As you are moving along your route, you see a horrific accident, or someone stranded alongside the freeway and think to yourself…okay God. I get it. Well, my "I get it moment" was approaching and I had no clue.

Chapter

The Perfect Storm

Not All Disasters Come with a

Warning.

When was the last time you got caught in the rain without an umbrella? Have you ever had to dig yourself out of your driveway in the wintertime? The answer to both questions is probably yes. In the northern parts of the United States people experience blizzards. The west coast endures earthquakes from time to time. The midwestern region has and will continue to go through its fair share of tornados. Down south gets drenched in water as the result of thunderstorms and hurricanes. I'm no meteorologist, but as a woman that watches the news, I'm aware that not all disasters come with a warning. Case in point, just a few days ago, residents of the southern parts of Texas were going about the day minding their own business. In the blink of an eye, the blue skies turned grey, and chaos struck which produced flooding along with tornados. It was unreal. Homes and businesses were destroyed. To think, just a few hours earlier, no one would have even thought to grab a raincoat when heading out the front door to start their day.

Unfortunately, storms are not solely tied to the weather. The wrong people can come into your life dressed like a beautiful Sunday morning and before you know it...boom! You're in the middle of a disaster. Let's just say my blue skies and green grass didn't last for too long.

One evening I went in to work just as I would do any other day. I was sitting in my cubicle when I received a call from someone I'd rather not name. Nevertheless, she questioned my identity as it related to my husband. Silly rabbit. She thought I was the girlfriend, but I let it be known that I was the wife; not that the title held much value if I was receiving this type of phone call. She proceeded to let me know that she and my husband had been dating for roughly eight or nine months. Imagine being eight years old at an amusement park. You're hopped up on drinks, candy, and all sorts of unhealthy delicate. You see the frog drop and instantly make a beeline for it. You know the ride that goes all the way to the top of the city skyline and drops you about a foot off the ground as fast as it can while you're strapped in, and your legs are dangling. There is a certain type of feeling you get in the pit of your stomach before you realize that you didn't slam dunk into the pavement. Well, my heart instantly dropped, and my stomach felt like the eight-year-old kid on the frog drop. I was trying my hardest to wrap my mind around this news, but the only thing I was left with was pure confusion. I tried to rationalize it. Maybe she had things mistaken is what I told myself in an effort to stop the bleeding, but that didn't work for long. This caller described in detail personal information that only a person close to our situation would know. She described the car my husband drove as well as the address to the home that we shared. Instantly, I needed to confirm if she had ever been to our home. Of course, the answer was yes. In her defense, she was under the impression that the home she frequented belonged to his aunt. The conversation continued to down the road of confusion because she never saw any family photos on the wall either. Remember, I mentioned earlier about the "I get it moment"? This was it. My light bulb went off and my life flash backwards for a quick second. The man of my dreams that caters to me and does nice things like sending just because its Monday flowers was a wolf in sheep's clothing. Now it made perfect sense why the house was always clean and in perfect condition upon my return from training. It was a cover-up, but he wasn't expecting God to reveal to me the blood on his hands. I didn't overreact with the young lady on the phone because clearly, she was just as clueless as I was about the entire situation. I clocked out of work and left for the day because I was in shock, shaking and my body felt numb. How could the man that helped pick up all the broken pieces of my life be the same man that broke me down? I informed him of the conversation I had earlier in the day and that's when the explanation started. He was apologetic, as he should have been. He confessed that he made a huge mistake, but it would never happen again. It took some time, but I accepted his apology and we remained married.

We both worked different shifts I was on days, and he worked overnight but we made it work. Over the years, I'd worked in various management positions then was offered a position out of State. We both agreed it would be an excellent opportunity for my career and a fresh start, so we decided to move. I accepted a position out of state in Lexington, Kentucky, and that's where life changed. I have never accepted failure as an option, so I went into the new job knowing it was a challenge, but I was ready. We packed up everything we owned and moved over 900 miles away from Texas with no family or friends; just the two of us. My daughter stayed in Texas to finish the school year. I thought this would be an amazing opportunity for us to grow closer and depend on each other.

Lexington, Kentucky was different, but I enjoyed the challenge on the job working as an Operational Manager at the University of Kentucky. After a few months, my husband hadn't found a job that he was satisfied with and wanted to move back home. I wanted to finish my contract before moving but he decided to move back anyway. I told him to go ahead of me and once my contract was completed, I would head back also. Distance does not always make the heart grow fonder especially when there are visible cracks in the foundation. Things got rocky with our marriage after he left. Communication became nonexistent. We'd be lucky to speak with each other once a week. Although I didn't set out to cheat on my husband, I did come across someone in Kentucky that made the time for me that my husband refused to make. This person gained my attention by showing me the love and attention that I was desperately missing. The tables turned quickly and before I knew it, I found myself in a full-blown situationship. We went out together and enjoyed life. It felt great until I got the most shocking news of my life. I found out I was pregnant and not with one baby but with twins. I immediately called my newfound lover to let him the big news unaware that he has some even bigger news of his own. He informed me that he was engaged. Yes, you heard me correctly...ENGAGED! To make matters worse, he had an entire wedding planned out and scheduled all while living a double life with me. Once again, I was faced with having kids without father present, but I refused to do anything other than be responsible for my unborn children.

Let's not forget that I was separated, but still married so I did feel somewhat of an obligation to at least mention this to my estranged husband. I would have rather he hear it from me than anyone else. Naturally, he was upset and needed some time to process the devastating news. I obliged. A few days had passed before he called to ask if he could come back to Kentucky for us to work things out. I was in disbelief but agreed. My husband wanted to raise the kids as his own and move forward as a family. How could I deny his such an honorable notion. We moved back to Texas before I gave birth to twin boys.

Life was wonderful. We were happy once again. My husband helped with every aspect of taking care of the kids. Things were heading in a positive direction. We both had great jobs and communication was better than ever. Everything else was water under the bridge.

I decided to follow my lifelong dream of opening my own childcare center and walk away from my cooperate job. My husband was less of a risk-taker. He preferred a job with a guaranteed paycheck and thought it was best to stick it out in my cooperate job rather than follow my passion for entrepreneurship. After a lot of persuasion, I was finally able to get my husband on board with my dream. I had my mindset and a solid plan to go with it. This was the turning point of my career and marriage all at once. I started the in-home daycare and money was tight because I no longer had a steady paycheck coming in. More of the financial burden was placed upon my husband. Although there were some detours and delays. the daycare was an absolute success. The only problem was an in-home center can only be licensed for twelve children. My headcount was maxed out but still didn't bring in enough income to match my cooperate job after processing overhead costs and payroll for my small staff. After reviewing my business plan with my husband, I mentioned that I needed to find a building if this was going to continue to make sense. Meanwhile, bills were getting behind because my husband moving to his own beat when it came to paying bills. He paid what he wanted when he wanted to.

Trying to keep the spark in our marriage going, I had a bright idea to bring lunch to my husband at work one night. Upon my arrival, I was told it was his night off. What do you mean, his night off? I was confused. Before I left, I made sure we were speaking about the same person. Yet again, I did not confront him immediately. This time I did a little private investigation work. My findings revealed that he was at a hotel, so I pulled up. After causing a scene I was asked to leave by the hotel staff. In that moment, I realized that the relationship I had given my all to was no more. Eight years of weathering the storm was flushed down the drain like it never mattered to him. Contrary to the previous statement, we did, however, remain married another year before the divorce button got pushed. The demise of our marriage could have been ugly, but we kept it as civil as we could for the kids. He was a huge help with the kids. I had just opened my daycare center with no start-up funds or money saved. Just a leap of faith. I knew that his help wasn't going to last forever, and it would be a challenge doing it alone, but I pressed forward despite it all. I was ready to finally stand on my own two feet and work through whatever obstacles that came my way.

Against All Odds   40

Chapter 3

Survival of the Fittest

Don't Go in the Water if You Can't Swim.

Everyone knows how the American fairytale goes. *Boy meets girl. The girl falls in love with boy. Boy and girl hold hands and run off into the sunset.* It sounds dreamy, but my story didn't end like that. Well, the first time around didn't. (I'm currently married to my soulmate, but I'll save that for another story) As previously mentioned, my husband (at the time) and I divorced after being married for nine years. I was forced to file for bankruptcy. It was a hard blow to lose literally almost everything that I worked so hard to acquire from the ground up. If I said it was a hard time in my life, that would be an understatement. Both of our vehicles were repossessed so I had to walk or catch a ride wherever I needed to go. Keep in mind, this was no small task since I had children to care for on top of it all. My situation could have broken my spirit, but my faith kept me pressing toward my dreams at the same time. Contrary to popular belief, I am a private person which is why no one knew what I was dealing with or how I was crying at the end of the day trying to figure out the next day's meal amongst other things.

There was never a moment of regret during the journey of entrepreneurship because I had a plan and I knew that the faith I clung to would help me to overcome every obstacle along my path.

I like to say that living life is like spending the day at an amusement park. Sound of your life you'll spend walking in circles due to distractions preventing you from getting to your destination or ride without a lot of veering. Other times you may be close to your dream, but the waiting period or line becomes too long for you deeming it unworthy of your time. There will be times when the ride is bumpy and would probably send you flying if it were not for the seatbelts while other times you can smile and laugh as you kick back and enjoy the cool breezes. The point I'm making is no one is exempt from the highs and lows of life so it's up to you how you handle it. There was a time when I was extremely traditional. If I couldn't feel it, I wouldn't read it. Unfortunately for me, that era has passed, and we're forced to live in a world built of technology. Everything is now virtual with no limit to the things we have access to.

One of the things I enjoy watching regardless of the type of day I'm having is motivational videos. I ran across a compilation video the other day that included Les Brown, Michael Todd, Steven Furtick, Jocko Willink, Eric Thomas, and Inky Johnson. I'll share the first few lines because the words set the stage for the remainder of the video.

"I don't care how good you are. I don't care how talented you are. I don't care how much you work on yourself. There are sometimes when things aren't going to go right.... Life happens. You can break mentally...spiritually...physically...and all of those are going to leave a mark."

Survival is a necessary tool that one must possess. How do you acquire such a tool? Never giving up is the short answer. There will be times when the world may appear to be against you. Keep the faith. There will be times when everything you thought was going right crumbles at the hands of one curve ball. Stay in the fight. Life is not always fair. You may even notice your personal life suffering from time to time.

Trust God. He's shifting things around to get you prepared for your breakthrough. Whatever you have to endure, just don't give up. Stand firm. Stand strong. Stay in the game. As I mentioned, I lost it all, my man, my money, and my support. But I am here today to tell you that I came back better than ever. I have an amazing husband, beautiful children, and loving friends and family that surround me. I no longer catch rides to take care of my business and my bank account doesn't need to be resuscitated. I sleep well at night because I know what the bottom feels like, so I give 110% every day to lower my chances of history repeating itself. I have learned to put my pride to the side and ask for help when needed. No one person can do it alone. From time to time, I take breaks to recharge and protect my mental health. If I'm not good, my family is not good. Take selfish moments if you must but just know that when you step your foot out of the door each day, you have two options: sink or swim. Even when the water seems rough, grab a surfboard, and ride the waves.

"Ask, and it will be given to you; seek, and you will find; knock, and it will be opened to you."

-*Matthew 7:7*

Chapter

Mirror, Mirror on the Wall

Be Careful What You Tell Yourself.

Words are powerful and should be utilized in the most cautious way. What you say to yourself is the exact thing your mind will begin to believe is true.

Over the course of our lives, we go through changes due to the many different experiences we endure. Some experiences hold the tendency to positively shape our behavior and thought processes, while others push us towards self-destruction. Come to think of it, many of the major changes in our lives have happened due to the woeful experiences we have encountered. In times of change, people grow more than they normally do in everyday, insignificant situations partially due to the imprint of destruction that is left in its wake.

There is a saying, "blessings come with testaments". One thing is for certain, you will face some obstacles in life. Most challenges will test your inner strength while others are less hectic. How you navigate your way through is based on what you've gained from the previous one. It is safe to assume certain situations will drag you through the mud and make you question your sanity level. Stand strong and stay in the fight. There is light at the end of the tunnel. Approach each experience with a sense of gratitude. If this were easy everyone would be doing it. Setting your priorities, following your action plan, and measuring your progress according to your timeline are things that will contribute to the outcome of your future in business.

As J.K. Rowling puts it, "*Rock bottom became the solid foundation on which I rebuilt my life.*" As you hit rock bottom, you really start to assess things differently. When everything in my life appeared to crumble at the same time including my finances and love life, I had to get a bird's eye view of the situation. Mentally, we can oftentimes visualize more waves in the storm than what is there which is why we should always approach each situation with clarity and a calm mind. Positive energy and conduct will trump chaos every time. Once I put these techniques into practice, I was able to navigate obstacles with a smile rather than tearing myself down for things that were meant to be learning experiences. In the present moment, I am still able to look back on past experiences and feel nothing but gratitude. I was finally able to walk the path destined for me with my head up and chest out. I don't regret any decisions I had to make. Adversity was my biggest lesson, but it definitely shifted my mindset on change. Change can be intimidating, but it is well worth it in the end. To be successful, a change in your mindset is vital. Despite the many external challenges, a positive viewpoint is going to empower you to gain more insights and grow freely, even at your lowest.

Let's review the life of one of the most notable media entertainment conglomerates in America...Walt Disney. His employment was terminated due to prejudgment. Walt Disney's employer assumed he lacked a creative imagination and could not offer ideas that would contribute to him being an asset to the company. Hindsight is always twenty-twenty. Walt Disney is now a household staple. Why do you ask? One word. PERSERVERANCE. Walt continued to press forward despite his current circumstances. He never gave up on himself. This is what he had to say about hitting rock bottom.

"All the adversity I've had in my life, all my troubles and obstacles, have strengthened me...You may not realize it when it happens, but a kick in the teeth may be the best thing in the world for you."

There are effective ways to help with getting back up after hitting rock bottom such as situational acceptance, trusting yourself and the process, and taking action. Acceptance is easier said than done. The mind can be prepared to accept reality while the heart moves at a slower pace. Truthfully, until both the mind and the heart are on the same page, healing is unrealistic. Human minds tend to hold on to adverse in turn holding people hostage to their own thoughts and emotions. The human mind has the ability to replay negative situations that avert individuals from moving forward. Hence, we find it just as difficult to accept the wrong in our lives and dwell on our mistakes. Acceptance is the key to leading a successful and content life. In order to do that, one must be willing to build trust within themselves as well as their mindset. Accepting the process of your life will encourage you to work toward personal development. As a result, motivation to expand your horizon, improve your skillset and test your limits is inevitable.

"Happiness can only exist in acceptance." – George Orwell

Being able to change what is in your control, accept what isn't and move forward will contribute to the type of life you will have in the future. In order to build trust with yourself, you must determine if the voice in your head is speaking in a positive light or a negative one.

Trust is a skill highly desired in the entrepreneurial world. Once trust is built, your outlook shifts, and your personal well-being becomes more of a priority than before. The trust stage is imperative because it sets the stage for you to unpack the next obstacle that arises. Don't misconstrue the messenger. I'm not saying that hitting rock bottom will be any less easy if it occurs again. What I am saying is that you will have the power and ability to see the best in yourself, be kind with your words, and know that this too shall pass.

Growth only comes in the wake of a lesson. In the entrepreneurial world, you have to be open to making mistakes. Unless you make mistakes and learn from them, it will be difficult to reach your full potential in this game. Many people get stuck in a rut due to the fear of taking risks, overlooking the potential of great outcomes.

In a situation where you think there is no way out, there lies an opportunity. Life doesn't just throw you failures and adversities, but it is up to you to leap over the storms and grab the positive nuggets. When you are consciously aware of your abilities and practice self-trust, you're able to pick out what is best for you.

When I started, I only had a direction...no resources or support in any form. I let my faith and my willingness to achieve my goals, guide me. My steps were slow and steady. I was brave and strategic. Most importantly, I trusted my gut. I decided not to allow failures to consume me. I aim for my goals and push through to the finish line.

Chapter

Murphy's Law

What Could Go Wrong, Will Go Wrong.

To bounce back up, you must be accepting of your situation. Only once you are willing to accept your situation can you truly work towards bettering it.

My life as a divorcee and single mother of three went downhill in no time. Caring for children with no outside help is hectic enough but try adding children with disabilities to the equation. Honestly, I didn't know if I was coming or going a lot of times. My twin boys were diagnosed with a disability called Intellectual Developmental Disorder (IDD). For those of you that aren't familiar with this disability, it limits and sometimes delays the ability to learn at a normal rate and level. IDD can impact the level of independent living that a person can have. I could have given up when juggling my parental skills to meet the needs of each of my children overwhelmed me. I could have even given up when I came to grips with the fact that from here on out, I had to get it out of the mud, but I didn't. Instead, it was at that moment that I realized I was not the only mother going through this level of adversity. I decided to pursue my dream of becoming an entrepreneur.

Despite my lack of financial stability, I was able to build and manage what I had started. My desire was to offer support to struggling and working mothers by providing a safe space for their children. Letting go of emotional baggage that was birthed from dark places is a breath of fresh air. It teaches us to accept what is and strive for a better situation. When I made the choice to let go of my grief, I was able to create a space for new ideas and opportunities. Only when the old foundation breaks down can you build resilience and find joy. As a struggling individual, the only favor you can do for yourself is accept full accountability for the choices you have made and grow from them. If you walk out of a storm without learning the lesson, you are doomed to repeat the storm again. Taking full control of how you operate and think will shape and transform your life as a whole.

Our mind has the power to influence our thoughts and behaviors. You can either train your mind to offer positive power and make effective changes in your life, or you can let that power control you. When an obstacle arises that appears to be more than we can handle, we tend to self-loath in our misery which is counter effective. However, if we train our minds to exercise their power positively, we can achieve what we are focused on. You have to continuously remind yourself that you are headed towards betterment and push your mind to stay just as positive for getting the results you want.

After being divorced, I was exposed to many challenges including having to find childcare for my twins while trying to make ends meet. It was a rough patch in my life, but my reality so I dealt with it. I knew that this was not the end all that be all so after reevaluating the way I was living my life, I made an action plan that would assist in turning the tables for the better.

When everything that could go wrong goes wrong, changing your vision allows you to view things from a different perspective. Ask yourself tough questions that will ultimately reveal problem areas that you need to work on. It is going to help you assess your progress and paint a clear picture of what you are capable of, where you are headed, and how you can reach the endpoint successfully. As Stephen Covey writes in Seven Habits of Highly Successful People, you should begin with an end in your mind. If you are unable to create a vision, a bigger picture of where you want to reach, you will not be able to grab your share of success. It can feel overwhelming to make fulfilling decisions based on your vision if you lack the dedication it takes to put in the work.

Once your vision is set, your action plan should be created next. What you need to do to get what you want is far more important than what will be the outcome. Consider internal controls, rather than external ones. Results may seem out of your control but all the actions you make for those results are fully in your control. Just breathe. Don't overwhelm yourself and take baby steps. Make short-term plans that yield positive results. Despite the magnitude of the results, stay consistent with your plan. You must continue working towards your goals, despite the external challenges. Once you get into the actions, do not turn back. This is where you apply pressure.

How you navigate this step will determine what doors can open for you. You won't always experience sunshine and roses. You must push yourself and move forward to bring a positive impact into your life. Constant improvement should stay at the forefront of your mind. By trusting your mindset, accepting your situation, and persistently working towards rewarding success, you will well on your way to success.

In the beginning, entrepreneurs face challenges and for many of them, the risk of their businesses' future can cause stressful triggers, possibly pushing them to the edge of mental and financial collapse. Not only can the future of a business become stressful but understanding the different components of a business can serve the same result such as lead conversion, finance management, operation management, and more. For any entrepreneur to capture success, good mental health is significantly important. More importantly, a mindset that drives you toward success and rational decision-making techniques that will provide entrepreneurs with an effective approach to business management.

Entrepreneurs are risk-takers. Most will bet it all on their dreams in hopes of winning big considering the amount of finances needed to get a business off the ground. Additionally, entrepreneurs have no certainty of income rolling in and/if their business will do well. The smartest way to lower the risk is by having an action plan and monitoring the progression of the business. Failure to do so will open the door for stress to grow.

Starting out, I evaluated and reevaluated my options, slowly putting the pieces of my puzzle together. I wanted to start small and gradually build my childcare center. Without a money machine backing up my business, my strategies had to be on point to avoid any foreseeable setbacks. Properly managing my remaining funds was just as important.

There were times when I thought things would crumble, but I didn't waiver. I stayed the course. My children were my driving force. I believed in myself, and I continued to press forward despite the opinion of others.

Putting into practice my new mindset changes contributed to my optimistic outlook on things. The views of others didn't carry as much weight as they used to. The more I leaned on myself and God, the less I worried. As I began to take stock of my progress, I realized that things were shifting for the good. Studies show that a new habit is formed in roughly two to three months which lined up perfectly with the changes in my life. I was able to pay my overdue bills. I started to sell lunch plates weekly to bring in extra income which supported my original business plan. I was then able to save enough money to purchase my own tax software for the next filing year. Just like that another business was born…my tax business. The income generated from my side businesses was invested in my childcare center. As the next tax season rolled around, I gathered enough funds to buy my first official brick-and-mortar for my childcare center.

I was focused on growth, and I focused on the available options that would help propel my business in the right direction. It was then that I realized we could do a lot more if we put our minds to it. My side businesses were getting me into the process of growth. It may be overwhelming to start out knowing that the only person responsible for the outcome of your business is yourself. However, if you continue to set goals and monitor your progress, you will continue to head toward the finish line.

My faith and ability to focus on my plan forced me to face struggles and finally get the results I desired. I had trained my mind to think in an optimistic manner because failure was not an option. Whenever I made a mistake, I went back to reevaluate it coming up with a new strategy every time something did not work out.

This process taught me one thing, one very important thing…to stay firm with my mindset and ignore the negative voices in my head. Even though the world is going to see your business as small, insignificant, and a temporary placeholder for bigger corporations, remind yourself that it is your learning and growing process. With a positive mindset, there is a lot you can achieve.

To this day, I have never forgotten the words from my pastor, Donny Flippo, "*you can, and you will succeed.*" He also spoke of the possibility that if a person came to you with a million dollars and all you need was a business plan, would you be prepared or would you have to get ready? At that moment, I knew I had to create a business plan. I had to grow, and I had to take action from now forward. I didn't think of finances, I only made two, five, and ten-year plans for my business. I had decided to keep my focus.

Starting out, many will question your choices and vision in an attempt to bring you down. Many will ask you to change your plan while offering up unwarranted criticism. Others will lend a helping hand when they can. But, in the end, it's just you and your plan. If you take control of your mindset and zone in on your focus, you will find success in the entire growth process.

Chapter

Back to the Basics

A Goal Without a Plan is a

Dream.

Waiting for the sun to shine again is a song a lot of people sing about life in general. It is arguably a common response that entrepreneurs dish out during a dry season in their business. While some business owners are drowning in the throes of life, waiting on a glimpse of hope, others are choosing to rebuild and redevelop due to the mindset that they possess. There is no right or wrong way to handle tough situations. However, you can reduce the downtime if you minimize the wallowing and take action on the things within your control.

But, is it worth waiting? Is it worth longing for the day when your pain will lessen by itself? After an ending phase of life, is it in your best favor to sit still and let life process everything for you?

Human life is complicated, and so are our experiences. One after another adversity pushes us to think it was always only our fault. After hitting rock bottom emotionally, physically, or professionally- many find themselves in a rut of hopelessness and many others break themselves free from their past. Here are a few ways that helped me get back to the basics when pressing forward from the trials and tribulations of life.

Changing My Outlook

The first step to changing the way I lived my life was to change my perspective and thought process while committing to being 100% transparent in everything that I did. I had to acknowledge that doing things the old way would push me back into the same rut that I was fighting so hard to get out of. Visualizing and making a change in how you want your life to only occurs after you make the decision that change is necessary. Once you make a decision, it is imperative that you have to stay firm and content with it. Allow success to be your driver and progress to be your ruler. Continuous monitoring of your progress and making the necessary adjustments will all things to shift in your favor.

It only takes a new perspective, a new approach to achieving your everyday goals and your long-term goals. When willing to rebuild and redevelop your though process and approach to life, you will have more room to identify priority goals and what changes you need to make in life.

As things began to shift in my life in a positive direction, I failed to condition my mindset. As a result, I kept getting the same results. No different than weight loss journeys. If you do not condition your mind to think differently, yes you might lose the weight, but I guarantee it will come back. Luckily for me, it didn't take me long to determine my mindset was not where it needed to be, so I worked on that area of my life. Once I had that facet of my life figured out, the game changed forever.

Although my family benefited for the changes that I made, I mostly did it for myself; to make myself proud. I now know that my past was not a failure, but a lesson for me to follow a new roadmap to success. I started out by evaluating my present state. I questioned myself. What is it that you want to do? What outcome do you want out of it? Have you trained your mind for the goal you are about to set? I knew having to answer those questions would be tough, but necessary. I did not let doubts infiltrate my mind. I stayed positive and committed to the process. It's understandable, you can never change anything unless you invest your mind and energy in it. While you may have the power, resources, and support, with a weak mindset, you will not be able to land the outcome you desire.

Allowing Room for Grace

When restarting, many changes and new strategies will bring in new results. Some results may not come in your favor. Do not let failed results discourage you. Allow yourself to make mistakes but be open to learning from each lesson. Go back and evaluate where you went wrong, you can then change your approach or alter your plan in congruence with your desired result.

Focus On The Present

Instead of feeling uncertain about your goal, or stressing about future results, remind yourself of the present moment. Encourage yourself to invest your positive mindset and skills in what you are doing right now. Stressing for your future today will do you no good. It will deprive you of the energy that is needed at the moment.

Finding My Motivation

While it may seem like you cannot keep your life from falling apart, remember that you must live in the moment and work on achieving the step-by-step goals you have set for yourself. You will have to commit to a strict schedule and protect your peace at all costs.

Starting out, I had days when I felt as though I was not meant to do this and should give up. However, I remembered my reason for starting. Seeing my kids smile served as the fuel I needed especially on the days when the horizon was filled with fog.

Life is better lived when you're surrounded by people who genuinely want to see you achieve your goals. Do not feel compelled to explain your goals to others as they will not always understand the vision. As long as your goals are comprehensive to you, that's all that matters. Stay focused and allow your talents to shine bright for the world. See you at the top!

Chapter 7

The Power of

Manifesting

Trust the Process.

Have you heard the story in Genesis 42:13 of the Bible where Joseph's brothers go to Egypt?

The scripture says, *"And they said, your servants were twelve brothers, the sons of one man, who lives in the land of Canaan. The youngest is now with our father, and one is no more."*

Joseph and his brothers went to graze their father's (Jacob) flock. During the journey, Joseph's brothers concocted a plan to kill Joseph and cover it up by stating that an animal had attacked him. However, what they didn't bank on was the survival of Joseph after the brothers left him to rot in an empty cistern. Instead, when one of the brothers return to the cistern, Joseph was gone. Sadly enough, they stuck with their lie, not understanding what truly happened to Joseph. Fast forward a few years. Jacob sent his remaining sons down to Egypt to buy grain, so they didn't starve to death during the years of famine. Ten of the twelve brothers took the journey. The younger son, Joseph's full-blooded brother, stays with their father, and Joseph is assumed to be dead. When the brothers arrive at their destination, they were met by whom they thought to be a stranger. Joseph beckoned for one of the brothers to bring him the younger brother while the rest of them were held captive in prison. Upon the return of the brother, Joseph revealed himself and they were in total shock. Joseph's brothers didn't know that the one they were speaking to was actually the dead brother they left in the empty cistern, nor did they know Joseph was the governor of the land.

Imagine being hated on because you were a dreamer who strived to have a better life than what you were living. Most individuals are pre-wired to accept the fact that not everyone will root for them. However, the negativity stings more when it comes from within your own circle. Joseph's brothers despised him for two reasons; he was a dreamer who saw passed the trees in the forest and they felt as though their father loved Joseph more than them. Perception can have you inching your way toward the cliff if you're not careful. Jacob loved all his sons equally and Joseph's dreams always included his brothers living the good life with him. Unfortunately, Joseph's brothers were too caught up in their own self-misery to see it that way. Ultimately, Pharaoh caught wind of Joseph's abilities to interpret dreams and asked for his assistance. Joseph interpreted Pharaoh's dream spot on and became the ruler of Pharaoh's land. The moral of this story is if you continue to trust and be faithful to God, he will make thy enemies your footstool. Sometimes people don't recognize the new you because *they didn't expect you to survive the fire!!* Let's break this down. Manifesting can be defined as creating things from nonexistence to reality by way of thoughts and beliefs. With that being said, Joseph had a vision that no one could see except him. Did he allow fear and judgment to distort his views? Absolutely not! He continued to show up as his best self and press toward the mark. Eventually, manifestation transpired. View it from the other side of the coin. What if Joseph would have listened to his brothers? He might have thought to himself, "Man, I'm tripping. Who am I to think I can interpret the thoughts of others that were created out of slumber?" He might have even laughed at himself about the entire situation. BUT GOD! A lot of times we are headed in the right direction with our God-given talent, but we are distracted by people and things that serve no value in our lives. Now…we're clear on the fact that Joseph's passion was manifested into fruition for the entire land to witness, but what about Joseph's brothers? The mere thought that his brothers were okay with Joseph being dead is troubling. What makes the situation mindboggling was the fact that Joseph being dead, did not change their life for the better. Be careful whom you share your intimate thoughts and dreams with. Not everyone is striving to be better than you. They just don't want better to happen for you. In my Tami Roman voice, *get into it!* At the end of the day, manifestation is not the end all be all. It is the gateway for opportunities. Joseph wasn't crowned governor of the land so he could kick off his sandals and eat manna all day. He earned a position that required even more work than he was initially doing.

Much like Joseph, you must be consistent and put in the work it takes to sustain what you have been blessed with.

Many people ask me what happens when the cameras snap the last photo, the curtains close and the lights go off. My answer is simple…I work. The grind is not always pretty. As a matter of fact, it's not pretty at all, grimy and gruesome is more like it. Please do not be fooled by the facade that social media attempts to paint. Social media is a platform utilized by the vast majority to highlight the celebrations, but never the work put in behind the scenes. My normal day consists of making sure my children have everything they need to start the day, along with the help from my husband. Once that task is checked off of my list, I check emails. I'm not going to lie either, depending on the type of week I've had, often times I'm checking emails before my feet even touch the floor. From there, I have meetings, contracts, travel planning, business partners, and speeches to juggle. The days aren't easy for me. Sometimes I do great at the balancing act and other times I suck, straight up.

If I can be transparent with you, reaching the "top" is not the difficult part. Maintaining success is where most people struggle, including me. Holding steady is a vicious cycle of rinsing and repeating, but the reward of it all is priceless. Now I could run down a blueprint for you to follow and sell it as a surefire way to reach success. However, as I mentioned previously, success looks different for everyone, but if you follow the basic steps, previously mentioned, you are guaranteed to be well on your way.

Do not give anyone permission to mute your voice because they cannot handle the sound of your strength. You have worked hard and fought for every ounce of it. That storm that you thought was going to take you out is the very thing that's going to push you through to victory. God is about to put you in rooms that didn't seem possible, and you can't act like you don't belong. Trust the process and I'll see you on the other side!

Chapter 8

Think About It

How Do You View Things?

If you have made it this far, congratulations on making the decision to stay in the fight. The upcoming pages are intentionally left blank for the sole purpose of notetaking and reflecting. As I wrap up my story, I pray that you have gained some sense of knowledge on how trying, yet amazing following your dreams can truly feel.

Below are questions that I would like you to ask yourself as you either start or continue your journey. This is an excellent tool that can be looked back at to measure your progress so be truthful and again, congratulations. I pray you have found my story to be a light of hope for you.

1. List your short-term goals for the next twelve months.

_____

_____

_____

_____

_____

_____

_____

2. List your long-term goals for the next five years.

_____

_____

_____

_____

_____

_____

_____

_____

3. List some of the potential obstacles that could prevent you from achieving your goals.

_____

_____

_____

_____

_____

_____

_____

4. Are any of the obstacles listed above preventable? If so, how will you handle those situations?

_____

_____

_____

_____

_____

_____

_____

5. How passionate are you about the goals that you have listed above?

_____

_____

_____

_____

_____

_____

_____

6. Timelines allow goals to stay consistent & on schedule. Jot down what that looks like for you (i.e. beginning stage, completion deadline, etc.).

_____

_____

_____

_____

_____

_____

7. Think back to a time in your life when all hope seemed to be gone. How did you overcome it?

_____

_____

_____

_____

_____

_____

8. Why are written goals more powerful?

_____

_____

_____

_____

_____

_____

_____

9. How can I align my goals with my values?

_____

_____

_____

_____

_____

_____

_____

_____

10. What is the difference between a goal and a wish?

_____

_____

_____

_____

_____

_____

11. Write out what you would like your blueprint to look like. Visual reminders tend to help you see the overall picture.

_____

_____

_____

_____

_____

_____

_____

12. It's inhumanly possible for one person to do it all. List the names of your closest supporters. Lean on them when you need motivation and encouragement.

_____

_____

_____

_____

_____

_____

<u>NOTES</u>

_____

_____

_____

_____

_____

_____

_____

_____

_____

_____

_____

_____

_____

_____

_____

_____

_____

_____

_____

_____

_____

<u>NOTES</u>

_____

_____

_____

_____

_____

_____

_____

_____

_____

_____

_____

_____

_____

_____

_____

_____

_____

_____

_____

_____

_____

_____

<u>NOTES</u>

_____

_____

_____

_____

_____

_____

_____

_____

_____

_____

_____

_____

_____

_____

_____

_____

_____

_____

_____

_____

_____

_____

_____

<u>NOTES</u>

_____

_____

_____

_____

_____

_____

_____

_____

_____

_____

_____

_____

_____

_____

_____

_____

_____

_____

_____

_____

NOTES

NOTES

"For where two or three gather in my name, there am I with them."

Matthew 18:20

Made in the USA
Middletown, DE
12 March 2023